African Religions

Ancient Traditional Beliefs
and Practices

Table of Contents

Introduction

As the title implies, the topic of this book is the different religious practices originating from Africa. Some African religions show similarities in beliefs and practices. However, as you'll soon learn, different African territories and their cultures have been home to many different religious beliefs. Each historical African territory has its own tale to tell and traditions that accompany it. While some are unchanged, others have adapted to the changing times.

These belief systems play a crucial role in the spirituality of African nations throughout their history. They allowed them to express and maintain their spiritual heritage in good times, even the most trying ones. You'll also learn that besides the differences stemming from cultural backgrounds, African religions were also influenced by Christianity, Islam, and other belief systems introduced to

African people from other parts of the world. However, the colorful African beliefs have also left their mark on other religions.

The following chapter will give you a sneak peek into African cosmologies and creation myths. It sets out a thorough explanation of the role of the Supreme Being and the myth of creation in different African religions. Moving on, you'll be introduced to some practices and rituals associated with ancestral worship and reverence. The dedicated chapter will provide beginner-friendly instructions on how to do these practices. Likewise, you'll also receive tips on how to practice divination, use oracles, music, dance, and storytelling, or perform communal worship and celebrate festivals as are traditional in African religions.

The last chapter discusses the ethics and morality of African religions. It showcases the different ethical and moral values incorporated into African belief systems and how these concepts shape individual and communal behavior among devotees. It will also introduce you to the concept of justice and its role in African religions. Last but not least, you'll learn about the importance of ethical codes and how they have evolved.

As you can see, this book promises to take you on an epic journey through African myths and beliefs, exploring the colorful backgrounds and ideas behind traditional African religions. The knowledge you gain by reading this book can be a great stepping stone into a more in-depth exploration of any of the religions. Even if you're only interested in learning a few traditional practices, the practical instructions will teach you how to incorporate these into your everyday life. If you're ready to commence this journey and expand your knowledge about African religions, don't hesitate to read on.

Chapter 1:

Introduction to African Religions

Despite their many similarities, there is a surprising number of different African religions. African belief systems can be broadly divided into two categories, autochthonous and introduced religions. The former incorporates indigenous beliefs originating from the continent, while the latter refers to Christianity, Islam, and other religions brought to Africa from other parts of the world.

Traditional African religions incorporate practices, symbols, and rituals revolving around cosmology, society, art, and so much more. For the devotees, their practices represent a way of life. It's part of their culture and societal norms and shapes their worldview. Due to their significant role in the lives of devotees, African religions are not homogenous nor stagnant. They're constantly evolving under the influence of cultural change, as well as the introduction of new traditions for other religions. They are also influenced by changes in generational views and technological developments. This is the main reason for their vast number in the first place.

There are over 50 countries in the African continent, each of which is further divided along tribal lines as well as traditional, cultural, and historical differences and influences. While some of these different territories are governed by the same belief systems, a wide array of variations exist between their practices. African religions are based on lived experiences. Each culture experiences different shifts and needs for expressing its faith and traditions. No African religion has doctrines for rituals and ceremonies. The practitioners of each religion perform these acts the way their ancestors did based on their experiences. Lead by their own needs, the younger generations add something to the ancient practices while still staying true to their ancestral heritage.

This chapter will discuss some of the most widespread African religions, including their diversity, history, and role in African societies. You'll also learn about the importance of African religions and the interaction between African religions and other religions.

Popular African Religions

Africa has the most colorful religious makeup of all continents. The number of religions existing in Africa is incredibly high and is still expanding. That said, here are some of the most widely practiced African religions.

Akan

The Akan religion has a unique view of deities. While being polytheistic, unlike many other traditional African religions, which have only one omnipotent deity who oversees other, lesser deities and people, the Akan belief system has a trinity of super-divinities. Onyame, the female Supreme Being, is associated with plentitude, the rain, and the Moon. Onyankopon, the second higher divinity, carries a male energy and is the counterpart of Onyame, representing the sun. The Akan religion unites these two essences into the third divinity, Odomankoma, which embodies their combined energies and the power of their bond. Devotees can call on either of the supernatural beings for protection, guidance, and more through prayers and charms. However, even more often, they address lesser deities and spirits in solitary and communal practices.

The concept of Odomankoma has an enormous role in its followers' lives. They credit this power for the creation of the universe, balance in people's lives, and the existence of natural and supernatural beings. They praise it regularly through uplifting community rituals that serve as a reminder of the power of unity. The lesser beings also help people connect to nature and spirituality. The presets, who act as intermediaries between the devotees, the deities, and spiritual guides, are held in high regard in the community.

Igbo

The Igbo religion hails from Southeast Nigeria and governs the lives of the Igbo people. Unlike other African religions, Igbo has strong foundations rooted in faith. The beliefs of Igbo people revolve around the creator named Chukwu (also known as Chineke), who is celebrated through regular rituals for health, guidance, and prosperity. They also venerate Ala, the earth goddess, and several other deities and spiritual guides. Ancestral spirits also play an enormous role in their lives as they are believed to be the greatest guides besides the creator.

Another reason the Igbo religion is more faith-based is that it has become heavily influenced by Christianity. Just like Christians, the Igbo people have adopted certain doctrines and centralized views about spirituality and faith. However, due to cultural differences predominant in the different territories, the religion is not uniform throughout the area; the Igbo people are separated into several cultural divisions, which are the northeastern, northern, western, southern, and eastern cultural divisions.

Yoruba

As one of the most well-known African religions, the Yoruba belief system centers on the idea of Ashe, the universal energy hosted by all things in nature. This powerful life force is given to living beings by the creator Olodumare. The Yoruba people live their lives in a way that allows them to follow their destiny (called Ayanmo) and reach a state of spiritual enlightenment that leads to unification with Olodumare.

Yoruba is rooted in Western Africa and is the most practiced religion in Toga, Nigeria, and Benin. Due to the slave trade and migration, the Yoruba religion also conquered several African diaspora regions. Nowadays, more and more people of African descent in Western countries are empowered by Yoruba spiritual practices. It allows them to experience life on a spiritual level and encourages them to follow their goals.

Serer

The Serer religion is centered on the deity Roog (or Rog), the creator and a merciful and omnipotent being. This deity is the embodiment of all female and male energies and can help with all matters in life. Devotees also have strong beliefs regarding life, death, cosmology, time and space, and ancestral spirits. They believe in the immortality of the soul and find reincarnation an ultimate goal for the living. Besides Roog, Serer practitioners often call on their ancestral spirits, as they believe these to be the intermediaries between the world of the living and the spiritual realm. They find it crucial to stay faithful and connected with the ancestral divine messengers, allowing these beings to guide them through their lives. They also worship lesser deities, spirits, and other supernatural beings by making offerings at sacred places in nature or shrines erected in their homes or communities.

Vodou

Vodou (also known as Voodoo) is an ancient religion originating from West Africa. Widely practiced in Benin, Togo, and Ghana, Vodou is based on belief surrounding a unique pantheon of deities who communicate with people through spiritual possession. In ancient times, animal sacrifice was also a fairly common practice, but it has become less popular due to the influence of other religions.

The coastal line of West Africa was a critical point during the transatlantic slave trade, as many slaves left Africa through it. They took their religious beliefs and traditions with them, including Vodou practices. Although somewhat influenced by local religions and Christianity, Vodou practices lived on through the next generation in the diaspora regions, including Brazil, Cuba, Haiti, and Louisiana.

Christianity and Islam

Although not traditionally African religions, Christianity and Islam deserve an honorable mention as they have become two of the most widely practiced religions in Africa. Christianity has been present in Africa since the 2nd century AD. Soon after it arrived in Northern Africa, Christianity took over people's lives, leaving an indelible impact. It soon becomes pervasive across the entire continent.

On one hand, the influence of Christian beliefs was seen as positive as it helped empower people through knowledge (via general education and literacy), leading them to take better care of themselves. On the other hand, the strong influence of Christian beliefs on native traditions led to a great deal of suppression of ancient African traditions. Fortunately, instead of completely erasing the traditional cultural makeup, it was only kept hidden - for people to discover them again.

Islam has the third largest number of practitioners in Africa. After arriving in North Africa in the 7th century, it soon took over the Northern and Western parts of the continent. Unlike Christianity, Islam hasn't put much pressure on traditional beliefs, which is why it has become so widely adopted by people across Africa.

The History and Role of Religion in African Societies

Religion has been crucial to people's lives in Africa since ancient times. Whether honoring ancient African religious beliefs, practicing Christian traditions, participating in a Muslim pilgrimage, observing the Sabbath, or doing anything else as part of their religion, African people emphasize their belief systems. They allow them to guide their lives, obtain their spiritual and personal growth goals, and honor those they believe can help them with these quests.

The ancient African societies were built around religious practices like honoring the faith of the community, oral traditions passed down to younger generations, and teaching others how to follow or celebrate certain religious principles. For thousands of years, the African people used religion to find answers to questions about the origin of the world, the reason behind people's existence, and events that had enormous impacts on people's lives.

In the different religions, they also found answers to questions related to death and the spiritual world.

In many African countries, religious practices and traditions are protected by law because society has found it crucial to preserve them. Freedom to follow whichever religion people prefer is also protected, and people who don't wish to honor any particular religion (or honor several) are also accepted in African societies. Consequently, the rainbow of different cultures and religions has not only managed to survive the test of time but also thrive and diversify through history.

Due to the increasingly large number of different spiritual practices, the African people learned to accept each other's differences and learn about other traditions around them. Christianity, Islam, Hinduism, traditional African religions, and Judaism all play their parts in African societies, as they have coexisted for hundreds and sometimes even thousands of years. Traditional African religion has become increasingly popular once again, many years after its spread from the Northern and Western parts of the continent. Once the ancestors from these parts reached South Africa, they already started to co-mingle with those carrying elements of Christianity and Islam.

Religion and spirituality in African societies have a role of this magnitude because these elements can be used to create a greater understanding of each other's differences. Instead of setting people aside due to their religious difference, African spiritual practice encourages people to live in harmony and has done so since all those religions started to co-mingle.

Traditional African religions are passed down through oral traditions. This way, older generations impart wisdom, traditional values, and the ancient way of life to the generations that follow. Rather than being taught as general tenets, African societies envelop these principles into myths, stories, and lore that has been circulating since ancient times. Due to this, the elders have highly distinguished roles in African societies. They are seen as authority figures, guides, and counselors and command respect.

African religious communities are made of people who share and celebrate the same traditions and practices. Individual members strive to be valuable to their community, as their beliefs dictate they can only exist and thrive spiritually within their community. In many African religious communities, being separated from one's community is viewed as a death sentence or even worse. Even if a community member moves far away, they are still influenced by the other members.

Religious beliefs in African societies are also based on moral order. This creates a sense of security within a specific religious community. Members are encouraged to follow moral codes and to live in order and harmony. They can receive guidance on how to live morally from their ancestral spirits. They can also turn to spiritual leaders, including pastors, priests, and other highly respected practitioners. These leaders have a crucial role in the survival of religious practices and are responsible for helping their communities thrive. Besides prayers and similar passive spiritual practices, some African societies also embrace traditions like spiritual healing, divination, and spiritual guidance led by deities, spirits, and other mythical beings.

Some believe that the ancestral spirits were once traditional healers or guides, acting as priests or other forms of spiritual guides for their communities. Just as they do nowadays, the ancient guides underwent years of training in spiritual practices. Through these, they've gained the wisdom and skills that allowed them to help those in need in the community. Besides healing and general spiritual guidance, some traditional community leaders are also trained in practices like finding hidden objects - something that's welcomed in modern times.

African societies practice ancestral veneration at every major event in a person's life - from weddings to births to finding a job. The entire community makes offerings to the ancestors and expresses their gratitude for the success of one or a few members. The creator doesn't receive as much attention because, in African societies, it's widely believed that people aren't worthy enough to address this Supreme Being. The ancestral and other spirits are used to communicate people's wishes to the creator. However, this is only practiced when the community falls on particularly hard times, experiencing events that could threaten their existence.

The Importance of African Religions

African religions are inextricably linked to traditional cultural practices. Not only did the different cultures leave their mark on religious practices, but the latter also influenced African cultures. And their influence didn't stop at the African continent either. It was carried to wherever African people migrated and established new communities.

In African societies, there is a triple cultural heritage - indicating the influence of traditional African religions, Christianity and Islam, over the different cultures. While many devotees of African religions have converted to Christianity or Islam in hopes of finding a better path in life, not all have given up their old customs. They carried them into their new social and economic environments across the world.

The transatlantic slave trade allowed the influence of African religions in societies to become global. They inspired the development and growth of blended cultural and religious traditions like Candalombe or Santeria. Nowadays, more and more people find solace in African religions in Western countries. The importance of converting to African religion has become widely acknowl-edged. The African diaspora has played a critical part in growing this acknowledgment, but now there is an equally large number of devotees who travel to Africa on pilgrimage, hoping to connect with the ancient traditions. The number of revival groups attempting to keep African religious prac-tices alive has also grown across the globe.

Women play a fundamental role in African re-ligious traditions - another aspect that significantly influenced people's lives. The many female deities honored in African religion helped empower wom-en, making them embrace inner gender roles and dynamics. In African religions, the male deities have female counterparts, giving women rights and a special place in African societies.

African religions incorporate a great sense of morality - much of it is derived from wisdom that allows people to live in harmony with their envi-ronment. Consequently, these belief systems have much to offer in terms of environmental protec-tion and making the world a better place for future generations.

Chapter 2:

African Cosmologies and Creation Myths

The word cosmology is derived from two Greek words, "cosmos," meaning universe, and "logos," meaning science, so it is defined as the science of the universe. African cosmology refers to how people contemplate and perceive the world around them and its impact on their lives and values. It reflects their search to find the purpose and meaning of life. African cosmology connects everything about people's lives like their morals, ideas, norms, rules, rituals, mythology, folklore, rites, social conduct, and philosophy.

The African universe consists of two separate realms - the spirit realm and the physical realm. They only have one supreme deity who lives in the heavens and is the most powerful being in the universe. Humans reside in the physical realm, which is under the control of the deity, yet they play a significant role. If African cosmology was a triangle, God would be on top, mankind at the center, and the spirit of the ancestors at the base. This reflects human beings' position on Earth between the sky or the heavens where God and the Orishas reside and the underworld where the spirits of the dead roam. It also shows the central role they occupy in the universe. Although the three worlds are separate from each other and consist of different beings, they are still connected and are constantly interacting with one another, mainly through the Orishas.

One can't talk about African mythology without mentioning the divinities or Orishas as they are called in religions like Yoruba, Santeria, Ifa, and Voodoo. Orishas are spiritual entities that some religions consider deities or demigods, while others consider them helpful spirits. In Yoruba, they are considered avatars of the supreme deity Olodumare.

There are an infinite number of Orishas in the universe, and each one of them is responsible for a specific domain. For instance, Shango is the Orisha of thunder, Oshun is the Orisha of love, and Yemaya is the Orisha of the ocean. There is a belief in Yoruba, Ghana, and other places in Africa that these divinities are regarded as the children of the Supreme Being. He didn't create them, but they came from him. This would explain why he entrusted them with the universe and the creation of human beings.

In Yoruba, the supreme deity is often regarded as distant and isn't concerned or aware of the lives of mankind. Since he lives in the heavens, he is so far away that he can't hear people's prayers or cries. He is also powerful and massive, and the simple human brain can't comprehend him. So, he created the Orishas, who are lesser beings yet powerful. They are inferior to God but superior to mankind. They act as mediators between God and humanity, they listen to their prayers and complaints and deliver them to the supreme deity. They also assist people with all aspects of their lives. Since human beings also have many petty problems that God can't be concerned with, the Orishas usually handle these issues by providing support and guidance to them.

In the Yoruba hierarchy, the Orishas are right under Olodumare, which reflects their significance. They also play a prominent role in the creation of the universe and mankind, and without them, human beings would have never been created.

There are two other types of divinities that also influence mankind: the spirits of the ancestors, which will be discussed in detail in the next chapter, and the forces of nature. There are spirits that reside in various places in nature, like lakes, rivers, forests, hills, and mountains, and can impact people's lives in different ways. For instance, a river spirit can cause drowning, or a mountain spirit can cause an accident.

African Cosmology is anthropocentric, meaning that human beings have a more central role in the universe than the supreme deity. So, everything that happens in the world is connected to them. African people believe that God, the Orishas, the spirits of the ancestors, and nature all exist to serve mankind. In Yoruba, human beings can only be understood based on their relationship with the Creator, and in Igbo, people and God are linked together since the spirit of the creator runs through them.

The Myth of Creation

At the beginning of time, before mankind was created, there was only marshland, sky, and water. Olodumare ruled the sky, and Orisha Olokun ruled the area below. The Orisha Obatala, who would become the father of mankind, took a look at the universe and felt that it was lacking something. There was more to be added to it to make it more alive and less dull. He went to Olodumare to ask for permission to finish creating the universe, and the supreme deity obliged.

Obatala wanted to create dry land for all creatures to roam freely on it. He went to Orunmila, the Orisha of wisdom and divination, to ask for his help. Orunmila told him he would need a palm nut, a black cat, a white hen, a snail shell filled with sand, and a long golden chain that he would use to travel from the sky to Earth. All the other Orishas provided Obatala with enough gold to make his chain. Orunmila supplied him with the rest of the items, and Obatala put them in his bag and was ready to go on his journey.

Obatala put his bag over his shoulder, bid Orunmila farewell, and started climbing down the chain. However, he discovered on his way that the chain was shorter than he expected, and he still had a long way to go. Orunmila was watching him, and he quickly told him to pour the sand from the snail's shell and toss the hen. The hen landed on the sand and began scattering it around, creating dry land, hills, and mountains. Obatala landed on one of the hills, which he called "Ife." There was now dry land everywhere on Earth.

Obatala dug a small hole and planted the palm nut, which grew instantly. It dropped other nuts, which also grew right away. Now Obatala created the universe. He built a hut and stayed on Earth to enjoy his creation with the black cat to keep him company. Although Obatala was proud of everything he had achieved, he began to feel bored after a few months. He was alone on Earth, so he decided to create human beings.

He dug in the soil until he found clay which he used to create mankind. However, after working for some time, he started to feel tired, so he took a break and drank wine that he made from the palm he had grown. He drank so much that he was intoxicated and wasn't aware of what he was doing.

Obatala ended up creating deformed figures. He called on Olodumare to breathe life into them.

The next morning, Obatala saw his creation and realized what he had done. He was consumed with guilt and vowed never to drink again and to become the protector of the deformed. To this day, Obatala is recognized as the guardian of the disabled.

The new people began building houses like Obatala's, and Ife soon became the first civilized village in Yoruba. The other Orishas were watching Obatala's creation, were very pleased with the result, and often visited him on Earth.

This is the creation myth in the West African Yoruba religion. However, there are other variations in each African tradition. Some share similarities with this myth, while others are different, but the premise is always the same.

Ife Creation Myth

The Ife creation myth shares many similarities with the Yoruba myth, with a few exceptions. Olodumare resided in the lower part of heaven, and he was the one who wanted to create dry land and sent Obatala with all the items to carry out his task.

After Obatala created dry land, he climbed up the golden chain to notify Olodumare that he finished his mission. Olodumare sent a chameleon to earth to confirm that dry lands were created. He then named Earth "Ife," which means "scared house." Olodumare gave Obatala the power to create mankind and gave Yemaya different sacred powers since she was the mother of the Orishas. He then retired to the upper part of heaven.

Santeria Creation Myth

In Santeria, Olodumare created the universe and then distributed different domains among the Orishas. Mankind developed a bond with the Orishas and communicated with them through sacrifices and rituals.

Voodoo Creation Myth

The Voodoo supreme deity Gran Maître created Damballa, the sky father who created mankind and the universe. Damballa is depicted as a black serpent. He used 7000 coils to create valleys, hills, plants, and stars. He then shed his snake skin to create water on Earth.

Efe Creation Myth

In Efe, Congo, the chief deity and the moon created the first man from clay, then God covered him with skin and let blood flow into his body so he would come to life. The deity whispered to him to have many children, and they can live their lives and eat from the many blessings God provided, but he and his offspring should never eat from the Tahu tree.

The human had many children, and they all followed God's rule. Even when he grew old and went to heaven, none of his children touched the tree. Later, they also became old and retired to heaven.

One day, there was a pregnant woman who was always curious about the Tahu tree. She told her husband that she desired nothing more than fruit from it, but her husband refused because he knew it was a forbidden tree. However, she kept persisting, so he gave in and went to the forest to pick fruit for her. It was late at night, and the husband thought no one would see him, but the moon was watching, and he told God right away. He was furious and killed all mankind. The story shares some similarities with Adam, Eve, and the forbidden tree, which is common in the Abrahamic religions.

Interpretation of the Creation Myths

One thing that all creation myths shared was that the creation of the universe wasn't a random act. In all religions, God represents order, so everything was organized and went according to plan. He first created the heavens, the sky, and the spiritual world; then, he created the Earth and mankind. For instance, in the Yoruba, Ife, and Efe God had already created the heavens and the spirits before the rest of creation. The stories also reflect mankind's central role in the universe because everything was created for them. Even the Orishas exist to assist humanity.

Although none of the stories mentioned what existed before God created the sky and heavens, it is common knowledge in African traditions that there was nothing and no one except the supreme deity. So, he created the universe from nothing. He didn't use any materials or transform one thing into another; he created the universe.

The name of the Supreme Being differs in many religions, but one name they all use to refer to him is the Creator. Even though the Orishas, moon, or spirits assisted in creating the Earth and mankind,

God created the universe before anything and anyone else existed.

The Significance of the Creation Myths

Creation myths play a prominent role in African beliefs, showcasing the significance of everything God created. For instance, in many religions, Earth is the mother Goddess since she is the home and protector of mankind. God created her before human beings to reflect that they can't survive without her, but they were created before animals because they have a bigger influence on the universe.

Every story has a beginning and an end. Human beings were created in the middle of the story. The creation myths explain how the world began and what it took to bring everything humans take for granted to life. There are many lessons that you can learn from these stories. For instance, the Yoruba myth shows the dangers of intoxication and how Obatala took responsibility for his actions and made up for them. The Efe story explains how people should always follow the Creator's rules, or there would be dire consequences. The universe isn't chaotic; there are laws and orders that one can't break whenever they please.

The Supreme Being

In African cosmology, God isn't just an idea. He is real and present in people's lives. Although some religions, like Yoruba, consider the supreme deity distant, some scholars disagree and find him present in people's lives and play a significant role as well. In religions like Mende, Akan, and Yoruba, the supreme deity is a male, while in the Ewe religion, the deity is a female. Other religions consider God both masculine and feminine and use the pronoun "they" to refer to them. He goes by different names in every religion, In Yoruba, Ifa, and Santeria, he is called Olodumare and Olorun, and in Voodoo, he is called Gran Maître. Since each religion is different, their concept of a deity differs as well; each reflects the people's lives and culture. However, the gods share similar characteristics that transform them from being an idea to concrete facts.

He is a real god who is aware of people's lives, listens to their prayers, and comes to their aid. In all religions, God is unique, he is unlike any other creature, and no one can match his power. He is the one in control of the universe; even the Orishas can't act without his permission. Without him, the universe would fall apart, and mankind would cease to exist. The supreme deity is also the creator of the universe. In some religions, he was the one who directly created it, while in others, he sent the Orishas. However, in all myths, he was the one who breathed life into mankind and gave them a soul. Although the Orishas played a huge role, they wouldn't have been able to finish the task without the supreme deity's permission, and none of them had the power to create the human spirit of their own accord.

God is also described as a king in many African religions since he controls the universe. He is often called the chief deity, and in some religions like Yoruba, he is referred to as Oba Orun, which means "the king in heaven."

His power is limitless, and nothing in the universe takes place without his knowledge, and he can do the impossible. He is described as omnipotent in some religions, like Yoruba and Igbo.

Everything has an end in the universe, except for God, since he is eternal. He doesn't have a beginning and will never cease to exist. The Yoruba people often compare him to a rock, as he never dies. They also believe that God is the one who will judge mankind for their actions, punish bad people for their mistakes, and reward the good ones for their virtue.

Cosmology and mythology are the foundation that ancient Africans built on their traditions and religious beliefs. They reflect the role of the Supreme Deity, the divinities, and mankind in the universe. They also give you a better understanding of your faith and roots.

Chapter 3:

Ancestral Worship and Veneration

Our ancestors were once human beings who led heroic or extraordinary lives and turned into divine spirits after they died. In other words, they were good people who led honest lives without harming or deceiving others. They were knowledgeable and highly respected in their communities, and the people often sought their guidance. Their lives were meaningful, and they died naturally at an old age and had a proper burial. Although they can be men and women, male ancestors play a more significant role in African religions since they are the patriarchs of the family.

Even though ancestors play a role that can seem divine and are worshiped by many people, they aren't considered deities in many religions. For instance, in the Yoruba hierarchy, they come after the supreme deity Olodumare and the Orishas. However, there are people who believe that their ancestors are as powerful as gods. It is a fine line that separates these spirits from the divine, and people can sometimes treat them as gods, especially since they have the power to bring prosperity or curse human beings.

Favors aren't the only reason the living worship and venerate their ancestors; it's also out of respect for their elders who once walked among them. These spirits and their descendants usually share a special bond since they come from the same lineage, as people usually worship the spirits of their dead family members like a great-grandparent.

The living has one goal in mind, to lead an honorable life so they can become ancestors after they die. For this reason, many people aren't afraid of death as they don't see it as the end but as the beginning of eternal life. They will roam freely between the physical and spiritual worlds and develop a deep connection with all other beings.

The Role and Significance of the Ancestors

In Yoruba and Ifa, the ancestors are called Egún. A different pronunciation of the same word means bones. The double meaning indicates how the spirits are connected to the bones of the descendants, which emphasizes the strong relationship between the living and the dead.

The ancestors exist everywhere in nature, like in the forests, air, rocks, mountains, trees, water, and caves. Although the living can't see them, they are there watching over their loved ones and providing them with guidance. However, they can appear to their family members in dreams, during divination, or in visions to tell them about good fortune coming their way or to warn them against impending doom.

Ancestors have a huge influence on people's lives. They help them in different ways, like providing assistance or offering advice. However, they usually ask for something in return for all the blessings they bestow. They expect their descendants to keep their memory alive, build shrines for them and keep them maintained, and present offerings.

The ancestors are usually kind and giving, but if the living neglects their shrines, they will curse them with misfortunes like illnesses by lifting their protection of them. However, they don't cause any major harm, just minor diseases to act as a reminder to be grateful for the gifts the ancestors continue to provide or a warning when the descendants stray from the right path.

This indicates that ancestors still experience human emotions and can get angry. However, their anger is never misplaced. They always feel responsible for their descendants, and like any parent, they sometimes feel the need to discipline their young, especially when they make big mistakes like breaking the law.

Ancestors play a prominent role in ancient African traditions and communities. They influence every aspect of people's lives, from searching for firewood to birth, weddings, and even deaths. They have special powers that they didn't possess when they were alive, like the ability to communicate with the divine and pass messages from him to the living. They can also send their descendants' prayers to god, and they deliver the answer to the prayers back to the living. In other words, one can communicate with the divine through them. They have the ability to understand the language of the deity and mankind.

The ancestors have other powers as well, which is probably why they are often mistaken for gods.

They can protect crops, provide good harvests, bring rain, cure diseases, and bless people with good health.

The living should cultivate a strong relationship with their ancestors by showing gratitude and asking for forgiveness when they sin. There are also certain rituals and practices to venerate, worship, and appease the ancestors so they continue their blessings over you.

Rituals and Practices

Your ancestors are all around you; some even say they are inside of their loved ones. They can share all your experiences, go wherever you go, and do whatever you do. You can communicate with your ancestors every day by performing specific rituals. You don't need special powers to connect with them; this ability is inside of you. It's your birthright since they are your blood and family. You can simply remember them and let your shared memories guide you. Parents and grandparents often train the younger generations to connect with their departed elders. There are various festivals that take place in Yoruba dedicated to the ancestors to facilitate communication with them. However, if you want to worship your ancestors in the privacy of your own home, build them a shrine.

Shrines

Make your ancestral shrine simple, especially if you are a beginner, as it will be easier to maintain. You can establish a connection with your ancestor through your shine then they will communicate with you through dreams or divination. Don't take the altar down or ignore it after the ancestor reaches out to you, or you will risk angering them.

Think of it as a memorial area where you will remember your departed. It is a place where you will reach out to your roots and ask for the guidance and wisdom of those who were here before you.

Instructions:

1. Choose a quiet room or space in your home to build your shrine. Make sure it's away from distractions so you can worship in peace and there are no kids around that can disturb the altar.

2. Make room for the shrine and clean the area, making sure it's spotless. In the Ifa religion,

clutter and dirt can bring negative energies and evil spiritual forces.

3. Cleanse the area with smoke like burning sage, cedar, or any other alternative. Light the leaves and fan them with your hand until they generate smoke.

4. It is better to cleanse the entire house as well, so take the burning leaves and spread the smoke into every room in the house while praying that all the negativity leaves your house for good. Make sure to set an intention first that you want to purify your home and remain focused on your intention until you finish.

5. Now, cleanse your body using the smoke from the leaves. Begin with the front of your body, starting from your toes to your head and then your back.

6. Seal the cleansed area with herbs and water to maintain the positive effect of the smoke. You can use the cascarilla plant or place a few drops of your favorite perfume in water; it should be a scent that you usually wear. Next, spit in the water to add your essence

so the spirits of the ancestors know that this is your shrine and that they should ask for your permission before entering.

7. Say a prayer on the water of what you are hoping to get from the shrine, like abundance, good fortune, long life, a stable home, or all of them together. Make sure to mention your first and last name before praying.

8. Sprinkle the water on the cleansed area while setting the intention in your heart that this will be a sacred space.

9. If there are ancestors you don't wish to invite into your shrine, make it clear that you don't want any communication with them. You can also add the names of the ones who are welcome. If you aren't familiar with your ancestors or don't know their names, simply think of the types of spirits you hope to attract to your shrine.

10. Now, you will prepare the shine by placing a table or box in the cleansed area and covering it with a piece of white cloth. Then, add a candle and a glass of water to create the four basic elements: air, water, fire, and earth.

11. Add pictures of your ancestors on the wall behind your shrine so you can remember them whenever you look at it. They will also remind you of their good character and contribution to their society so you can follow in their footsteps.

12. If you follow another religion like Islam, Christianity, or Buddhism, add their holy books to the shrine, like the Quran or the Bible.

13. Now, your shrine is ready for use. Light the candle and stand in front of the shrine.

14. Tell your ancestors this shrine is for them and that you will use it on a regular basis to pray and meditate. Don't make a commitment you won't be able to keep. For instance, don't say you will use the shrine every day when you don't have the time. You will break your word and anger the spirits. Stick with one day a week, so the spirits know when you will communicate with them.

Remember, the items you place in your shrine, like the pictures and candles, will attract the spirits of your ancestors to you. However, you have to keep recharging it by praying or meditating. If you only use your shrine when you need a favor or help, you will weaken the connection between you and your ancestors.

Present Offerings

Appease your ancestors by constantly making offerings to them at the shrine. Offerings create a mutually beneficial relationship between you and the spirits. You can't keep asking them for favors without giving something in return. Offerings are meant to honor and show your gratitude for your ancestors. For instance, an offering of food isn't meant to satisfy their hunger but to keep their memory alive by presenting their favorite food. In African tradition, people offer a small part of their every meal and place the plate on the altar or in front of it. It is preferable to use a cracked dish to symbolize their broken dead body that is no longer here.

Food offerings are necessary as they keep the spirits near, so make sure that there is always food at the shrine. Agree with the ancestors on the feeding frequency and keep your word. You can prepare a plate for them with every meal, or you can feed them once a week. Both are fine as long as you have a schedule and stick to it.

There are various other offerings you can make, like alcohol, tea, or coffee, which you can place with the food. The spirits will also appreciate cigars and flowers. After you connect with your ancestors, they will begin to make requests like a specific type of food, jewelry, sweets, etc. You must provide whatever they ask for to keep the line of communication open and avoid angering them.

Instructions:

1. Place the offerings at the shrine.
2. Express your gratitude to the ancestors for their continuing support and guidance.

Meditation

Meditation is an effective way to connect you with your ancestors, and you can easily do it at your home near your shrine since it's a cleansed and quiet area.

Instructions:

1. Light a candle and pray to your ancestors to provide you with guidance or messages. This

depends on what you hope to achieve from your meditation, whether you need help with a decision or you are simply preparing yourself to receive any messages from them.

2. Sit in a comfortable position, close your eyes, and free your mind from any fears or worries.
3. Breathe in and out deeply and slowly while remaining focused on receiving the message in a vision.

The Relationship between the Living and the Dead

In African traditions, the dead aren't really gone, so they should never be forgotten. They are all around you, waiting for you to find the right way to connect with them. Rituals and practices have a huge impact on your interactions with the spirits of your ancestors. You create a line of communication with them to send and receive messages to one another.

There are ancestors that you haven't met who died hundreds of years ago, you can benefit from their wisdom, but you need to find them first. Ask elderly family members about your older ancestors, like a great, great grandparent. Take their names, pictures, or any information you can find about them and use them in your rituals. You will be able to connect with relatives you never had the chance to meet and learn from their experiences. Remember that they are always watching over you, and they know you are their blood. They are calling on you and waiting for you to reach out to them to provide guidance and assistance.

Your ancestors are no longer with you in the physical world, but through practices and rituals, you will feel them near you. You will live your life knowing you aren't alone but supported and guided by the spirits of your dearly departed.

Worshiping and venerating the ancestors isn't magic or a demonic practice. It is a birthright running through your blood, a calling to your roots that you should answer. Whenever you experience misfortune in your life, think of what you have done to anger the spirits. Have you strayed from the right path? Have you neglected your shrine? Appease them right away so they continue their blessings and protection over you; you have a duty to your ancestors. Just like you need them, they also need you to worship them and keep their memory alive. So, give first, and you shall receive.

Chapter 4:

Traditional Religious Practices and Rituals

African religion is filled with traditional religious practices, rituals, and customs that form the cornerstone of their cultures and beliefs. This chapter dives into the fascinating world of traditional African spiritualism, exploring how music, dance, and storytelling significantly connect individuals to their faith. It provides an overview of the importance of community and a sense of belonging within the African religious culture through gathering around fires to perform ceremonies together. Furthermore, this chapter sheds light on all aspects of these ceremonies, taking an in-depth look at the symbols used by each region and understanding how they are used to create a deeper connection with religious principles.

Traditional African Religious Practices

Traditional African religious practices have been in existence for centuries. These practices often involve the use of supernatural forces, rituals, and ceremonies as part of worship. They serve as a way to honor ancestors and other spiritual powers while also providing a connection between the physical world and the spiritual realm.

The belief systems of traditional African religions revolve around creation stories that describe how humans were given certain roles by their gods or spirits. In some cases, these stories may include an original ancestor who gave life to humanity before they were sent off into the world. The idea behind these beliefs is that all elements of nature, including plants, animals, weather patterns, and spiritual forces, are connected to each other. Thus, traditional African religions focus on developing harmonious relationships with the environment and spiritual forces, as well as promoting justice in society.

In almost all traditional African religious practices, ancestor worship plays a pivotal role. Ancestors are believed to have special knowledge of the spiritual realm, and they can play a part in passing it down through generations. They are often venerated and respected for their wisdom, strength, and guidance. It is believed that they can intercede between humans and gods or spirits when it comes to matters of fortune, health, and other aspects of life. As such, ancestor worship is essential to many traditional African religions.

Rituals play a major role in traditional African religious practices. Often these rituals involve offerings made to gods or spirits to gain their favor or protection. Offerings can include food, animals, coins, and other goods. In addition to offerings, prayers are used to further honor the gods or spirits. Music and dance may also be included as part of these rituals.

Sacred sites are another aspect of traditional African religious practices. These places are often believed to have a special connection with spiritual forces that make them powerful locations for worship or rituals. Sacred sites may include natural features such as mountains or rivers, as well as man-made structures like shrines and temples. People visit sacred sites to pay homage to ancestral spirits and receive their guidance and protection.

In traditional African religions, divination is another tool used to gain insight into the future.

Divination practices vary between different cultures, but they often involve the use of objects such as shells or bones to determine what the future holds. Diviners interpret their findings and give advice on how to best address any potential issues or opportunities that may arise in the near future.

Initiation rites designed to mark milestones in a person's life are also part of African religions. They involve symbolic acts that signify an individual's passage from one stage of life to another. Examples of these rituals include coming-of-age ceremonies for adolescents and funerary rites for those who have passed away.

Overall, traditional African religious practices are deeply connected with nature and rely heavily on ancestor worship, rituals, sacred sites, divination practices, and initiation rites. These practices have been passed down for generations and still shape the spiritual landscape of many African cultures today. They provide a connection to both the physical world and spiritual realm while also promoting justice in society.

African religious practices should not be confused with modern-day religions such as

Christianity or Islam, which have become more pervasive in many parts of Africa over the last few centuries. While some aspects may overlap between these two belief systems, they are fundamentally different in terms of their religious teachings and rituals. Nevertheless, traditional African religions continue to play a significant role in the lives of many Africans today.

Role of Divination in African Religions

Divination is commonly used in African religions to help connect with the spirit world to gain a greater understanding of the journey of life. It helps to foretell future events, interpret omens, receive divine guidance, and even help heal physical and mental ailments. Divination practices are deeply embedded in many African cultures and are seen as a powerful tool for obtaining wisdom from ancestral spirits.

Revelatory divination, on the other hand, is used for understanding past misfortunes and relies on a wide variety of methods, including trance states. In this type of divination, the diviner is thought to enter a trance-like state in which they become possessed by a spirit or deity who then communicates a message. In southeastern Burkina Faso, for example, a spirit is said to have no tongue but communicates through hand gestures made by the possessed diviner. Other forms of revelatory divination include rituals like sacrifices where animals are sacrificed to please or appease spirits in order to receive their blessing and guidance. Folk healers commonly use divinatory techniques such as dream interpretation, scrying (seeing images in a pool of water), reading cards, and visiting seers who tell fortunes.

These methods are also used in larger sects that have become a critical part of African religious life over time. One example is the sect of Mwali from southeastern Africa which relies heavily on trances and spirit possession for guidance and communication with deities. Similarly, the Ngombo from the southern Democratic Republic of Congo uses animal sacrifices as well as consultations with prophets for revelatory purposes.

Role of Oracle in African Religions

Oracle is a vital part of many African religions, playing a significant role in both spiritual guidance and community decision-making. This long-held tradition has a variety of forms, from divination to healing rituals and more. In most African cultures, oracles are seen as a bridge between the mundane world and the spirit one.

In traditional African religions, oracles often take the form of objects such as bones, pebbles, sticks, and stones with markings on them that are used to divine information about past events, present problems, or future predictions. People would consult with the oracle by asking specific questions, which would be answered by interpreting the patterns on these objects. Oracular rituals could also involve mediums and ritual specialists who were believed to have conducted communication between human beings and the gods or their ancestors.

One of the most common forms of oracle is known as "Ifa" or "divine judgment." Practitioners use a set of sacred symbols to provide insight into people's lives and seek advice on how to navigate difficult times. They may use either cowrie shells or palm nuts that have been marked with special designs to determine the answers they get from their ancestors. This method is still widely practiced in West Africa today among many Yoruba-speaking people. According to this religion, each person is born under an odu – a sign determined by divination which is believed to represent their fate from birth until death. The odu was determined by consulting various oracle tools known as 'Opele' whereby different objects such as cowrie shells were thrown on the ground while prayers were said, interpreted based on their position after they landed on the ground, and later revealed its message related to one's life destiny.

The use of an oracle in many African religions goes beyond divination (fortune telling) but also involves healing rituals where sacred items such as talismans and amulets are used for protection against misfortune. A good example of this practice can be found in Yoruba culture, where people may wear beads with inscriptions believed to contain spells that protect them against harm caused by supernatural forces. All these practices show how the oracles have been deeply entrenched in African cultures for centuries and remain relevant today despite modern influences from other faiths or belief systems around the world.

Role of Music, Dance, and Storytelling in African Religions

Music

Music plays also plays a significant role ls, serving as an integral part of the spiritual experience. Music has long been used to invoke the presence of deities and ancestors and to foster a connection between the physical world and the spirit realm. It is also employed to facilitate sacred ceremonies, often in accompaniment with dance.

Examples of musical instruments used in traditional African religious rituals include drums, rattles, bells, flutes, and double-reed horns, known as adungu. Each instrument serves a unique purpose and can be heard throughout many different types of African ceremonies. For example, drums are typically used for deepening meditation or maintaining rhythm during worship services. Rattles are commonly used for ceremonial processions or shamanic journeys; bells are used in ritual healing. Flutes are played to invoke spirits or evoke trance states, and adungu often accompany songs dedicated to divinities.

The Maasai people of East Africa have perhaps most famously embraced the use of music in their spiritual practices. They use rhythmic drumming known as hudo to direct their energies toward their practice of ancestor veneration. The Ewe people of Southern Ghana, meanwhile, have crafted intricate rhythms using several different kinds of drums for their community celebrations, honoring the gods who protect them from harm. In Western Africa's Yoruba tradition, collective singing is thought to bring harmony between human beings and deities. On special occasions such as weddings or coming-of-age ceremonies, musicians often play drums and xylophones together to create grooves that induce communal dancing – a symbolic gesture expressing joyous appreciation for divine blessings bestowed upon them by higher powers.

Dance

Dance is an integral part of traditional African re-ligious rituals, and it has been used for centuries in various ceremonies, rituals, and festivals. In tradi-tional African belief systems, dance serves a num-ber of purposes. It is seen as a way to communicate with the gods and spirits. It is also used to honor the dead and celebrate events or milestones.

One example of dance being used in traditional African religious rituals is that of the kufutu ceremony from the Yoruba people of Nigeria. The kufutu ceremony uses singing, chanting, and dancing to invoke ancestral spirits. Participants in this ceremony also wear colorful clothing and masks, symbolizing their spiritual connections with their ancestors. By performing these dances, they hope to receive blessings from the gods or ancestral spirits.

Dance is also used to invoke spiritual forces from the natural world. For example, in some parts of Africa where rain and fertile soil are essential for survival, communities may perform a dance called the Ndiho before the planting season begins in order to ask for blessings of rain and fertility.

In another example, many African cultures use symbols that are associated with their culture's creation stories or cosmologies when they perform dances during religious ceremonies. For example, during Nyabinghi ceremonies held by Rastafarians in Jamaica and other areas, dancers use a circular formation known as a "ring play" that symbolizes unity among different generations while honoring their ancestors who were taken away during slavery times. Through such symbolic dances, participants strive to connect with their spiritual pasts while also celebrating their identities through movement.

Story Telling

The use of storytelling in traditional African religious rituals is a principal aspect of many cultures and beliefs. In these ceremonies, stories are used to pass down values and lessons and to explain the world around them. Stories can be used to explain spiritual beliefs and values or even provide a moral lesson.

In many African societies, stories have been passed down orally from generation to generation by elders and teachers, giving generations insight into their ancestral roots while providing them with moral training. These tales often serve as a way of teaching young generations about their culture, helping to instill values that will help guide their future lives.

One example of the use of story-telling in traditional African religious rituals is found in the Igbo tribal culture of Nigeria. In this culture, it is believed that gods can communicate through dreams and visions and that these visions should be shared with the rest of the tribe through stories. During sacred gatherings, elders would gather around a fire and exchange stories about their vision's journey with the gods - a practice known as 'Uwa Aha Ndi Igbo' (a festival for all Igbos). For example, during one such gathering, an elder might tell a story about one of their dreams involving a mysterious spirit who was trying to communicate some kind of message from the gods – this kind of story could be seen as both entertaining but also educational for younger members of the community.

Importance of Communal Worship

Communal worship and festivals are of great significance, as they enable communal connection and provide an opportunity for people to connect with the spiritual world. Communal worship and festivals unite different communities in traditions, beliefs, and culture. In traditional African religions, communal worship takes place around shrines and altars dedicated to particular deities or spirits. At these times, worshippers come to offer sacrifices, pray for divine intervention or protection, seek guidance, or perform rituals. During worship gatherings, participants sing sacred songs and invoke the power of the spirits they are honoring through prayer. This type of worship acts as a conduit between the physical world and the spiritual realm, enabling people to become more conscious of their own spirituality as well as that of their environment. Additionally, communal worship creates a sense of unity among worshippers.

Festivals also serve a vital purpose by providing a way for members of a community or tribe to celebrate special occasions such as harvests or seasonal changes. For example, during the Efik festival in Nigeria, people gather together to pay tribute to the gods they believe protect their land by offering food and drink offerings at shrines dedicated to various deities. Similarly, the Zulu Ukweshwana festival celebrates past victories over enemies who tried to invade their land by performing ritual dances throughout their villages accompanied by chanting and drumming music which serves as an expression of gratitude towards their gods for protecting them from harm.

There are many examples of how communal worship and festivals are practiced in African religions. In Yoruba religion, the annual Egungun festival is celebrated to honor ancestors and thank them for all that they have done for the community. During the festival, devotees dress up in elaborate traditional costumes as a part of a procession that moves through town. The event culminates with offerings being made to the ancestors and dances performed in their honor.

In Vodun (Voodoo) religion, the Dahomean Vodun ceremony is held annually to celebrate Ogun, the god of iron who represents strength, action, and creativity. During this ceremony, worshippers make offerings to Ogun by pouring libations on an iron knife or sword before proceeding with various rituals such as drumming, dancing, and singing songs dedicated to him.

The importance of communal worship and festivals in African religions cannot be overstated. Communal worship and festivals serve as a way for believers to come together and celebrate their faith, share stories, and strengthen their ties with one another. They also provide a way for those from different religious backgrounds to come together, learn about each other's traditions, and build mutual understanding.

Chapter 5:

Traditional Religious Ethics and Morality

African traditional religions have always been a source of intrigue and excitement. Many studies have been conducted on the ethical and moral dimensions within their religious worldviews, and the findings are quite interesting. The chapter in this book delves into this topic to explore the way in which traditional ethics and morality of these religious communities impact daily lives, both individually and collectively. It shows us how morals can vary within African traditional religions due to geographic, temporal, and cultural factors that cause certain values to be prioritized over others. It also looks at how religion has lent itself to protecting core values systems for many generations by adapting and evolution of traditional ethics. In this chapter, you will gain invaluable insight into the complexities of ethical systems within various African traditional religions.

The traditional African religions are diverse and rich in ethical and moral values. These values, codified into the laws of traditional religion, act not only as a set of guiding principles for individuals but also as a foundation of social organization for entire communities. By understanding these values, one can gain greater insight into how African societies function and how their beliefs shape individual behavior.

Ethical and Moral Values

1. Ubuntu

The concept of Ubuntu is also an important ethical value in African religions. Ubuntu is derived from an ancient Bantu proverb meaning "I am because we are," which emphasizes that individuals are not separate entities but rather part of a larger collective. It espouses the interconnectedness of all humans and their responsibility to act in ways that benefit everyone. Ubuntu stresses concepts such as empathy, compassion, respect for others, selflessness, and a sense of shared humanity. This value is closely linked to the communal nature of traditional African societies, where collective success was seen as essential for overall well-being.

2. Maat

Maat is one of the most important ethical and moral values of traditional African religions. The term Maat comes from ancient Egyptian religion and means truth, justice, and balance. This concept is often depicted as a goddess, symbolizing the importance of living in harmony with justice, truth, and order. These guidelines are believed to be necessary for successful life and happiness. They shape individual as well as communal behavior by stressing things like honesty, fairness, responsibility, and respect for others. An example of how this value affects behavior can be seen in most African cultures, where relationships between members of the community take precedence over individual gain or pleasure. In essence, upholding Maat serves as a guide to the right action; it requires devoting oneself to doing the right thing instead of the easy or personally beneficial thing. For the community to prosper, everyone must put aside personal interests while maintaining respect for others. Maat is believed to be upheld by a higher power that will reward those who are in harmony with it or punish those who go against it.

3. Ancestor Veneration

Ancestor veneration is an important part of many African cultures. It serves to reinforce familial ties among members of the community. Ancestors are seen as spiritual intermediaries between humans and the gods, able to mediate on behalf of their living descendants. They are believed to possess great wisdom and knowledge that can be accessed through rituals and ceremonies. Moreover, many Africans believe that ancestors are capable of intervening in the lives of their living relatives to help them succeed and protect them from misfortune. Respect for ancestors is a key moral value often emphasized in traditional African religions because it instills a sense of filial piety and gratitude toward one's ancestors and the community at large.

4. Communitarianism

Another common ethical value found in traditional African religions is communitarianism. In this worldview, individuals are seen as part of an interconnected community, with each individual playing an important role in sustaining its well-being. This concept emphasizes both collective responsibility and mutual support among members of a community, demanding that everyone work together to assure the success of the whole rather than focusing only on personal gain. This value is linked to the belief that each person's actions have a ripple effect on the entire community and, thus, should be carried out with consideration for the collective good. The emphasis on communal rather than individual success encourages cooperation, collaboration, and mutual aid among members of a community.

5. Hospitality

Hospitality is an important ethical and moral value that defines the traditional belief systems of many African religions. It reflects a deep-rooted reverence for community and respect among all people, regardless of race or religion. For example, in Asante culture, it is considered a moral obligation to offer refuge and sustenance to strangers and guests, as seen in their proverb: "It is a great shame for the fire not to be kindled and for the guest not to be welcomed." Such kindness affects not only individuals but also communities at large. Acts of hospitality bring people closer together and show recognition of cultural differences. This encourages openness to diverse perspectives and builds acceptance among African cultures. When hospitality is practiced, it strengthens community bonds while also preserving traditional values.

6. Respect for Nature

In traditional African religions, there is a great deal of respect for nature. Nature is seen as sacred and as having its own spirit or energy. This energy is often referred to as "umoya" (Zulu) and is believed to be present in all living things. Many traditional religious beliefs view humans as part of the environment rather than its masters and emphasize that we must work in balance with nature. This value emphasizes the importance of protecting resources such as water, land, air, plants, and animals to ensure collective survival. It also promotes sustainable practices such as crop rotation, reforestation, and waste management that support ecological health.

As such, humans should tread lightly on the earth and should not take more than they need from it.

7. The Importance of Ritual

Rituals are often seen as a way of connecting with the spirit world or with the ancestors. They can also be used for healing purposes or to bring about good fortune. Rituals often involve the use of symbols, music, dance, and chanting, and they are typically led by a shaman or priestess and are practiced with great reverence.

8. The Power of Words

Traditional African religions emphasize the power of words to shape individual and communal behavior, which is a concept that has shaped their culture for generations. The saying 'Speak it into existence' conveys this notion of the power of words; what you speak can shape your present reality as well as your future state. If one speaks positively and confidently with conviction, they will begin to see positive results in their lives. Individuals are encouraged to practice mindfulness in the words they use when they communicate with each other, as people must be intentional and mindful when delivering messages and instructions to create growth and harmony within a community. To take this idea further, speaking thought-provoking wisdom passed on from generation to generation creates unified communities with distinct African identities. It also keeps traditions alive through storytelling by elders or village chiefs, who use memorable anecdotes as teaching tools that shape individual values and collective behaviors, allowing for stronger cultural ties within traditional African societies.

9. Morality

In addition to these values, many African religions also emphasize morality. This includes concepts such as truthfulness and honesty, justice and fairness, courage and bravery, humility and respectfulness, piety and obedience, self-discipline and restraint, wisdom and prudence. These moral codes form the basis for social order within African communities by setting expectations for behavior both among individuals and between different groups. By understanding these core values that guide acceptable behavior in traditional African religions, one can gain greater insight into how their beliefs inform individual decision-making and their impact on the larger society.

Overall, African religious values serve as a touchstone for morality and behavior within traditional societies. Through their emphasis on respect for ancestors, communitarianism, and Ubuntu, one can understand how these ethical concepts shape individual decision-making in African communities and how they influence the larger social order. By gaining an understanding of these values, it is possible to gain deeper insight into African cultures and how their beliefs shape the contemporary world.

Concept of Justice in African Traditional Religions

Justice is a concept that is closely linked to morality and is seen as an essential element of social harmony and order. Justice is viewed as something that must be upheld in order to maintain balance and assure the well-being of the community. In many African societies, justice is seen as a way to right wrongs done against individuals or groups by providing avenues for dispute resolution through the practice of restorative justice.

Justice means different things to different African cultures. In some cultures, justice is seen as upholding communal values such as honesty, respect, and cooperation among members of the same group. In others, justice served to punish wrongdoers who violated laws or customs established by the community. In this case, punishments ranged from small fines or reprimands to more serious penalties such as ostracism or even death.

For example, in Yoruba culture from Nigeria, justice is based on a system of reciprocity known as "msulurumu," which means "pay for wrongs." This system dictated that if someone did something wrong to another person, then they had to pay reparations either through material goods or through labor. If this wasn't possible, then other forms of punishment were used, such as public humiliation or banishment from the community. The same principle applied to cases of theft where if someone stole something, they would have to pay back twice its value in reparation plus an additional penalty depending on what was stolen.

In addition to punishing wrongdoers and upholding communal values, traditional African religions also believe that justice should be balanced with mercy and compassion so that people don't become too harsh with their punishments while still maintaining order within the community. This balance between mercy and justice can be seen in many African belief systems, including Akan culture from Ghana, which states that "Ananse na nyame dua no," meaning humans and gods both have responsibilities when it comes to justice—humans are responsible for punishing wrongdoing while gods are responsible for showing mercy without judgment.

Overall, traditional African religions view justice as an essential part of maintaining balance within society by providing avenues for dispute resolution and punishments for wrongdoing while also taking into account mercy and compassion towards all those involved in a given situation.

Role of Ethics in African Religion and Its Evolution

Traditional African religions have an ethos, or ethical code, which abides in the harmony of human relationships with other humans and with the spiritual realm. The primary role that ethical codes play in traditional African religions is to preserve harmony within each other, as well as to uphold justice, fairness, respect for life, and protection of the environment.

Ethical codes evolve over time according to changes in society's values and beliefs. For example, members of traditional African societies once adhered to language-based taboos that were believed to control supernatural forces; however, these same societies later began embracing more abstract concepts like justice and forgiveness that could be applied universally across different cultures.

In the Yoruba religion of Nigeria, one oft-cited ethical code is that of "ma se ile" (translated as "let us do good"). This code emphasizes respect for others and individual responsibility, stressing the importance of carrying out deeds with moral consequences in mind. It also promotes justice, compassion, gratitude, and fairness while discouraging greed and selfishness.

In other areas, such as Ghana and Ethiopia, traditional African religions have evolved to include concepts like peacebuilding and reconciliation. These newer notions are based on the belief that peace can be achieved through cooperation between different factions instead of violence or war. Thus, ethical codes in these societies place greater emphasis on understanding each other's perspectives, conflict resolution, and empathy.

One of the most prominent examples of an ethical code from a traditional African religion is found in West Africa's Akan religion. This religion is based on the concept of Sankofa – a combination of two words that mean "to go back" and "to take," respectively – which symbolizes learning from the past to improve one's future. The Akan believe that understanding their history is key to building a better future for their descendants; with this view comes a strong sense of responsibility toward future generations as well as current generations who are suffering from injustice or neglect.

Understanding the ethical codes of traditional African religions can help people to appreciate the importance of community, respect for life, justice, fairness, and protecting the environment. Through these codes, adherents are able to foster a greater sense of unity with their creator. Evolution also serves as a testimony to how you must continuously reassess values in order to promote a more just and harmonious society.

Furthermore, ethical codes remind that individuals should abide by their moral conscience when making decisions and weigh them against long-term implications for both themselves and their communities at large. In this way, these ethical codes provide timeless lessons and guides towards making ethical decisions.

Overall, the role of ethical codes continues to be an important part of how Africans view their relationship with God and each other. The evolution from language-based taboos to more modern concepts like peacebuilding and reconciliation is a testament to how these values have adapted throughout history and still remain relevant today.

Ethics are key values and principles which govern the behavior of an individual or a group in any given cultural setting. In traditional African religions, ethical codes play a vital role in establishing and maintaining social order. A well-defined system of ethics provides guidance on how people should interact with each other, how to behave within the community, and how to treat the environment. Ethical codes are foundational for the stability and prosperity of a society, as well as the well-being of its people.

Conclusion

Every culture has its origins, history, and traditions that still influence its modern-day beliefs and lives. Although many people in Africa have adopted different religions like Islam and Christianity, some still hold on to their old faith and incorporate it into their new religious beliefs. This book covered everything related to ancient African traditions and practices to connect you with your roots.

The book first introduced the concept of African religions and explained each belief while shedding light on their diversity. It then took you back in time to witness the history of ancient African traditions and their impact on societies. The book also explored the significant role these religions play in African culture and their relationship with other faiths.

You can only learn about an ancient culture when you understand its mythology and cosmology.

The book took you into the mythical and enchanting world of ancient Africa, where you learned about the different creation myths in various African religions. It also explained the prominent role of Olodumare, the Supreme God, and their role in the creation of the universe. The book explored the different interpretations and variations of these myths and their role.

Ancient African beliefs didn't revolve around the worship of one deity. They also venerated their ancestors, who they held in very high regard and believed could provide guidance and blessings. The book explains all the different rituals and practices related to ancestral veneration and worship. It also discussed how these rituals could connect the living to the dead.

There are various other rituals and customs besides ancestral worship. The book covered these practices and introduced the concepts of oracles and divination in ancient African traditions.

Many of their rituals reflect their diverse customs, like music, dancing, and storytelling. The book delved into these rituals and their role within each religion. It also provided information about festivals and communal worship and their significance in African traditions.

The last part of the book explored the ethics and morality of African religions. It first introduced the morals and ethics associated with faith and their impact on the behavior of the community and the individual. The word justice can have different meanings in different cultures and beliefs. The book explains what this concept stands for in African traditions and its impact on society. It also covered the role of ethical codes in religions and their evolution over time.

References

(N.d.). http://file:///C:/Users/sarah/Down-loads/217834-Article%20Text-535653-1-10-20211123.pdf

African Traditional Religion. (n.d.). Org. Za. https://www.sahistory.org.za/article/african-traditional-religion

Burnett, J. (2004, February 9). Voo-doo and West Africa's Spiritual Life. NPR. https://www.npr.org/2004/02/09/1666721/voodoo-and-west-africas-spiritual-life

Chapter 3: Traditional African religious beliefs and practices. (2010, April 15). Pew Research Center's Religion & Public Life Project. https://www.pewresearch.org/religion/2010/04/15/tradi-tional-african-religious-beliefs-and-practices-is-lam-and-christianity-in-sub-saharan-africa/

Chiorazzi, A. (2015, October 6). The spirituality of Africa. Harvard Gazette. https://news.harvard.edu/gazette/story/2015/10/the-spirituality-of-africa/

Gyekye, K. (2011). African Ethics. In E. N. Zalta (Ed.), The Stanford Encyclopedia of Philosophy (Fall 2011). Metaphysics Research Lab, Stanford University.

Imoka-Ubochioma, C. (1638969143000). The Yoruba story of creation. Linkedin.com. https://www.linkedin.com/pulse/yoruba-story-creation-dr-chizoba-imoka-ubochioma/

Isidienu, I. C., & Onyekelu, A. C. (2021). Ancestral cults in African traditional religion: Their relevance in the contemporary African society. Journal of African Studies and Sustainable Development, 4(4). https://acjol.org/index.php/jassd/article/view/1409

Issa, N. M., Rossi, R., Alvarenga, R. K., & de Araujo, E. L. (n.d.). Oro a egún. ReVista. https://revista.drclas.harvard.edu/oro-a-egun/

LEGBA - guardian of the Crossroads - African burial ground national monument (U.s. national Park service). (n.d.). Nps.gov. https://www.nps.gov/afbg/learn/historyculture/legba.htm

LibGuides: African traditional religions textbook: Ifa: Chapter 5. Our ancestors are with us now. (2021). https://research.auctr.edu/Ifa/Chap5Intro

Lin, W. (2015). The dimensions of African cosmology. https://www.academia.edu/15521549/THE_DIMENSIONS_OF_AFRICAN_COSMOLOGY

Lin, W. (2015). The dimensions of African cosmology. https://www.academia.edu/15521549/THE_DIMENSIONS_OF_AFRICAN_COSMOLOGY

Mark, J. J. (2021). Orisha. World History Encyclopedia. https://www.worldhistory.org/Orisha/

Mark, J. J. (2021). Orisha. World History Encyclopedia. https://www.worldhistory.org/Orisha/

Molefe, M., & Maraganedzha, M. (2022). African Traditional Religion and moral philosophy. Religious Studies, 1–16. https://doi.org/10.1017/s0034412522000543

Morris, N., & Sansom, F. (2012). African Myths. Franklin Watts.

Mudzudza, S. (2015). Ancestor Spirits and their role in African Traditional Religion. https://www.

academia.edu/18969932/Ancestor_Spirits_and_their_role_in_African_Traditional_Religion

Ndemanu, M. T. (n.d.). Traditional African religions and their influences on the worldviews of Bangwa people of Cameroon: Expanding the cultural horizons of study abroad students and professionals. Eric.Ed.Gov. https://files.eric.ed.gov/fulltext/EJ1169262.pdf4

Nel, P. J. (2009). Morality and religion in African thought. Acta Theologica, 28(2). https://doi.org/10.4314/actat.v28i2.48880

Nwosu, O. S. (2004). Morality in African traditional society. New Political Science, 26(2), 205–229. https://doi.org/10.1080/0739314042000217061

Odozor, P. I. (n.d.). The Essence of African Traditional Religion. Church Life Journal. https://churchlifejournal.nd.edu/articles/the-essence-of-african-traditional-religion/

Odozor, P. I. (n.d.). The essence of African Traditional Religion. Church Life Journal. https://churchlifejournal.nd.edu/articles/the-essence-of-african-traditional-religion/

Olupona, J. K. (2022, December 1). 15 Facts on African Religions —. The Interfaith Observer. http://www.theinterfaithobserver.org/journal-articles/2022/12/1/facts-on-african-religions

Ost, B. (2015). LibGuides: Traditional African religions: Akan. https://research.auctr.edu/c.php?g=404402&p=2752856

Ost, B. (2015). LibGuides: Traditional African religions: Bantu. https://research.auctr.edu/c.php?g=404402&p=2752858

Parrinder, G. (1970). African Traditional Religion. Greenwood Press.

Pew forum on religion & public life / Islam and Christianity in sub-Saharan Africa. (n.d.). Interfaithalliance.org. https://interfaithalliance.org/wp-content/uploads/2018/07/pew-tradl-african-religious-beliefs-and-practices.pdf

Religion, E. O. (n.d.). The cult of ancestors: A focal point for prayers in African traditional communities. Ajol.Info. https://www.ajol.info/index.php/jrhr/article/view/87321/77037#:~:text=The%20

ancestors%2C%20or%20the%20living,could%20
be%20men%20or%20women.

Religions in Africa. (2021, January 30). Map-
pr. https://www.mappr.co/thematic-maps/
religion-map-africa-continent/

Richardson, S. (n.d.). Ancestor veneration: What
is it and why is it important? Urban Lotus Jewelry. https://www.urbanlotusjewelry.com/blogs/
musings/how-to-connect-with-your-ancestors

The Editors of Encyclopedia Britannica. (2018).
African religions. In Encyclopedia Britannica.

The Editors of Encyclopedia Britannica. (2018).
African religions. In Encyclopedia Britannica.

The Editors of Encyclopedia Britannica. (2021).
African religions summary. In Encyclopedia
Britannica.

Traditional African Religions. (2021, July
13). Set Free. https://www.setfreealliance.org/
traditional-african-religions/

Vaudoise, M. (2019, November 24). A ritual to reconnect with your ancestors.

Spirituality & Health. https://www.spirituality-health.com/articles/2019/11/24/a-ritual-to-recon-nect-with-your-ancestors

Walking Worlds. (2017). Divination and Oracles. Createspace Independent Publishing Platform.

Wedel, J. (2008). Santería. In Encyclopaedia of the History of Science, Technology, and Medicine in Non-Western Cultures (pp. 1923–1926). Springer Netherlands.

9 798215 868270